# Star Rangers
*Sci-Fi Plays*

by David Walke

## Contents

### Section 1
| | |
|---|---|
| Aliens | 2 |
| Dark Force | 7 |

### Section 2
| | |
|---|---|
| E.D. | 12 |
| Star Wards | 17 |

### Section 3
| | |
|---|---|
| Close Encounters | 22 |
| 3001 – A Space Oddity | 27 |

Edinburgh Gate
Harlow, Essex

# Aliens

| Characters | |
|---|---|
| **Captain Cosmic** – Star Ranger | **Kog** – Alien |
| **Kaput** – Star Ranger | **Alien Fighter 1** |
| **E.D.** – Electro Droid | **Alien Fighter 2** |

## SCENE 1

The Star Rangers' star-ship. The Rangers sit at the controls.

**Captain**   We are Star Rangers.

**E.D.**   We patrol the stars.

**Kaput**   We keep the Galaxy safe.

*(Voice from radio.)*

**Kog**   Help! Help me!

**Captain**   Who is it? What's up?

**Kog**   *(Radio voice)* My ship has been hit. I need help!

*(Kaput looks out of the star-ship's window.)*

**Kaput**   I can see him, Captain. He's over there.

**E.D.**   Beep-boop … hold on. I'll fly over.

## SCENE 2

The aliens' star-ship. Kog is on the floor.

*(Enter Star Rangers.)*

**Captain**   What's up?

**Kog**   My ship was attacked by bandits.

**Kaput**   Are you in pain?

**Kog**   No, the pain is in me. My leg is hurt.

**Kaput**   Let me see.

| | |
|---|---|
| **E.D.** | Boop-beep … you need a bandage. |
| | *(Kaput puts bandage on Kog's leg.)* |
| **Kog** | The engines are not working. |
| **Captain** | E.D., see if you can fix the engines. |
| **E.D.** | Beep-boop … OK, Captain. |
| | *(Exit E.D.)* |
| **Kog** | Thank you. I'm Kog. |
| **Captain** | We are Star Rangers. Always ready for danger! |
| **Kaput** | And always ready for a cup of tea. I'll put the kettle on. |
| | *(Exit Kaput. Enter E.D.)* |
| **E.D.** | Boop-beep … the engines are fixed, Captain. |
| **Captain** | Well done, E.D. |
| | *(Enter Kaput with mugs. They all drink.)* |
| **Kaput** | And well done, Kaput! |
| **Captain** | OK, Kog. You can go on your way now. |
| **Kog** | Thank you, my friends. I will not forget this. |

## SCENE 3

The Rangers' star-ship. Three days later.

                  (Alarm sound … WOOP … WOOP … WOOP …)

**E.D.**          Beep-boop … Red alert. Black star-ship coming at us fast.

**Captain**    It must be the bandits! Fire all guns!

                  (Gun sounds … ZAP … ZAP … BAM …)

**Kaput**      We hit it. It's stopped!

**Captain**    OK, let's beam over. Get your weapons ready.

## SCENE 4

On board the black star-ship. The ship looks empty.

                  (Transporter beam sound … ZZZZZZZ … Enter Rangers.)

**Kaput**      There's nobody here, Captain. The ship's empty.

**Captain**    No … there must be somebody here …

**E.D.**          Boop-beep … be careful. It might be a trap.

                  (Enter alien fighters.)

**Alien 1**    Drop your weapons!

| | |
|---|---|
| **Kaput** | Look out, Captain! |
| | (Gun sounds … ZAP … BAM … ZAP …) |
| **Alien 2** | Drop your weapons or we will kill you! |
| | (Gun sounds … BAM … ZAP … BAM …) |
| **Kaput** | Look out, Captain. The bandits are all around us. |
| **Captain** | I think we've had it, Kaput. |
| | (Enter Kog.) |
| **Kog** | Stop! Stop! Put down your weapons. |
| **Alien 1** | Yes, Master. |
| **Kog** | These men are my friends. They saved my life. |
| **Captain** | Kog? Is that you? |
| **Kog** | Yes! I'm sorry, my friends. My men thought you were bandits. |
| **Kaput** | But *we* thought *you* were bandits. |
| **Kog** | It was a bad mistake for both of us. |
| **Captain** | Yes, we nearly killed each other. |
| | (Alarm sound … WOOP … WOOP … WOOP …) |
| **Alien 2** | Master! A large battleship is coming at us fast. |
| | (Kog looks at screen.) |

| | |
|---|---|
| **Kog** | That's them! That's the bandits. |
| **Kaput** | Wow! Look at the size of their ship. We can't beat that. |
| **Captain** | Rubbish! We are Star Rangers. Come on, let's beam back to our ship. |
| **Kog** | I will attack from this side, my friends. You attack from the other side. |
| **Captain** | Together we will beat them. |
| | *(Beam sound … ZZZZZZZZZZ. Exit Rangers.)* |

## SCENE 5

*The Rangers' star-ship. The Rangers are at the controls.*

| | |
|---|---|
| **Kaput** | Here they come! Bandits! |
| **Captain** | OK, men! Blast away! |
| **E.D.** | Beep-boop … fire all guns. |
| | *(Gun sounds … ZAP … ZAP … BAM …)* |
| **Kog** | *(Radio voice)* Look out, Rangers! Bandits behind you! I'll get them. |
| | *(Battle sounds … ZAP … BLAM … BOOM …)* |
| **Kaput** | The bandits are hit. Kog hit them! |
| **E.D.** | Boop-beep … bandit ship destroyed, Captain. |
| **Captain** | Thanks, Kog. You saved *us* that time! |
| **Kog** | You saved *me* last time. That makes us even. |
| **Captain** | Goodbye, Kog. We'll meet again. |
| **Kog** | Goodbye, Star Rangers. |
| **Kaput** | And goodbye bandits! |
| **E.D.** | Beep-boop … Star Rangers are GO! |

# Dark Force

### Characters

**Captain Cosmic** – Star Ranger  
**Kaput** – Star Ranger  
**E.D.** – Electro Droid  
**Varg** – Dark Force Leader  
**Dark Force Trooper**  
**Narrator**

## SCENE

The Star Rangers' star-ship. Captain Cosmic sits at the controls.

**Narrator**   Star Rangers patrol the stars, always looking for danger.

**Captain**   Where's my breakfast, E.D.?

*(Enter E.D.)*

**E.D.**   Beep-boop … here it is, Captain.

*(Cosmic drinks from a mug.)*

**Captain**   Yuk! This tea isn't fit for a pig.

**E.D.**   Boop-beep … sorry, Captain. I'll get you some that is.

**Narrator**   *(Alarm)* WOOP … WOOP … WOOP …

*(Kaput runs in.)*

**Kaput**   It's a red alert, Captain.

**Captain**   What's the problem?

**E.D.**   Beep-boop … It's an enemy ship, Captain.

**Kaput**   It's coming at us fast.

*(Cosmic looks out of the window.)*

**Captain**   Oh, no! It's a Dark Force ship.

**Kaput**   Fire the blast guns!

**Narrator**   *(Guns)* VOOM … VOOM …

**Captain**   Let's get out of here fast!

**E.D.**   Boop-beep … maximum speed, Captain.

| | |
|---|---|
| **Narrator** | *(Engines)* VROOOM … |
| **Kaput** | Look out. It's firing back at us! |
| **Narrator** | *(Guns)* BAM … BAM … BAM … |
| **Trooper** | *(Radio voice)* Star Rangers. Stop! |
| **Captain** | Come on E.D. Faster! Faster! |
| **Kaput** | It's no good, Captain. The Dark Force ship is bigger than us. |
| **Trooper** | *(Radio voice)* This is Dark Force. Stop, or we will blast you to bits. |
| **E.D.** | Beep-boop … what shall I do, Captain? |
| **Captain** | Cut the engines, E.D. He's got us. |
| **Trooper** | *(Radio voice)* Put down your guns. Our leader will beam onto your ship. |
| **Captain** | Get ready, men. We'll jump on him. |
| **Kaput** | I'll bash him to bits. |
| **Narrator** | *(Beam)* ZZZZZZ … |
| | *(Enter Varg.)* |
| **Varg** | Stand back, Star Rangers. I am Varg. I am Dark Force. |

| | |
|---|---|
| **Kaput** | *(Whispers)* He's very big, Captain. |
| **E.D.** | Boop-beep … and he looks very mean. |
| **Captain** | *(Whispers)* Yes … em … maybe we won't jump on him just yet. |
| **Varg** | I want your star-ship, Star Rangers. |
| **Captain** | Why do you need our star-ship? |
| **Varg** | I am going to attack Star Base. |
| **Kaput** | No! You can't attack Star Base. |
| **Varg** | Yes I can. I will use your ship to get into Star Base. Then I will blast Star Base to pieces. |
| **Captain** | That's evil! |
| **Kaput** | It's a bit sneaky, too. |
| **Varg** | Silence! Get ready to blast off. |
| **E.D.** | Beep-boop … so you are going to hide on our ship? |

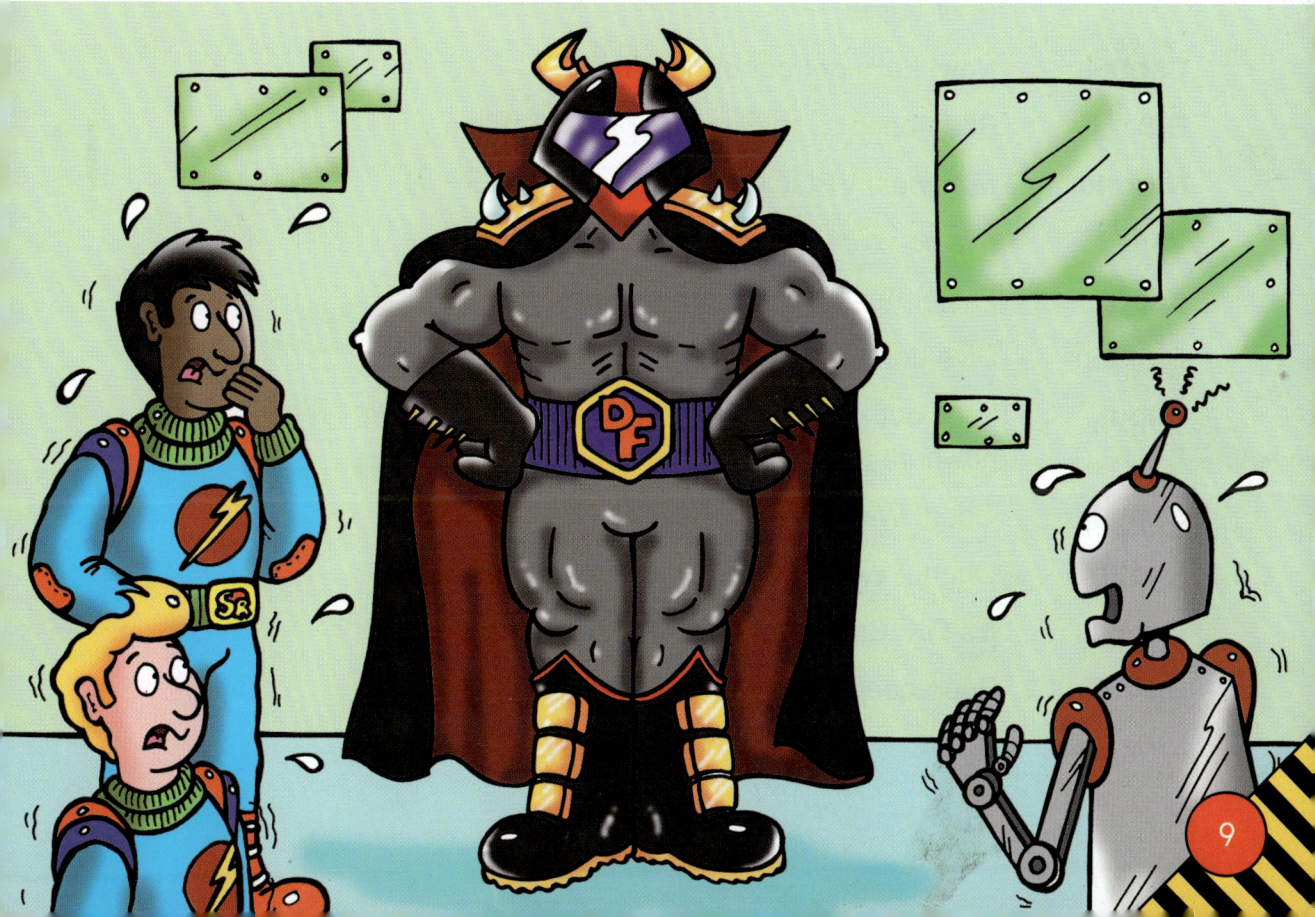

| | |
|---|---|
| **Varg** | Yes. When I'm inside Star Base my men will attack. |
| **E.D.** | Boop-beep … but the new Star Base is underwater. |
| **Kaput** | *(Whispers)* What's E.D. on about, Captain? Star Base is not underwater. |
| **Captain** | *(Whispers)* I know, but just play along. |
| **E.D.** | Beep-boop … Can you swim, Varg? |
| **Varg** | Er … no … I can't. |
| **Captain** | You will never get into Star Base if you can't swim. |
| **Kaput** | Have you got arm-bands, Varg? Arm-bands will help you swim. |
| **Varg** | I think I may have some on my ship. |
| **E.D.** | Boop-beep … beam back and get them. |
| **Varg** | OK. Don't try to get away. I'll be back. |
| **Narrator** | *(Beam)* ZZZZZZ … |
| | *(Exit Varg.)* |
| **Captain** | Now! Let's get out of here fast! |
| **E.D.** | Beep-boop … maximum speed, Captain. |
| **Narrator** | *(Engines)* VROOOOM … |
| **Varg** | *(Radio voice)* Hey! Star Rangers! Stop! |
| **Kaput** | Faster, E.D. Varg's coming after us. |
| **Captain** | Dive down to that planet, E.D. I've got an idea. |
| **Kaput** | Look out! This planet is all mountains. There's nowhere to land. |
| **Captain** | Good! Watch this! |
| **Kaput** | Oh, no! We're going to hit that mountain. |
| **Captain** | It's OK. Can you see that gap in the cliffs, E.D.? |
| **E.D.** | Boop-beep … I'm going for it! |
| **Varg** | *(Radio voice)* You'll not get away, Star Rangers. |

| | |
|---|---|
| **Captain** | Hang on! |
| | *(Rangers fly through the gap.)* |
| **Narrator** | *(Engines)* VROOOOOOM … |
| **Kaput** | We made it! |
| **Varg** | *(Radio voice)* Aagh! No! |
| | *(Varg crashes.)* |
| **Narrator** | *(Crash sounds)* VROOOM … CRUNCH … |
| **Captain** | Varg's crashed. His ship's too big to get through. |
| **Varg** | *(Radio voice)* You smashed my star-ship. Come back. I'll get you! |
| **Captain** | Bye, Varg. We win! Star Rangers are GO! |

# E.D.

| **Characters** | |
|---|---|
| **Captain Cosmic** – Star Ranger | **Santon Guard 1** |
| **Kaput** – Star Ranger | **Santon Guard 2** |
| **E.D.** – Electro Droid | **Narrator** |

## SCENE 1

The Star Rangers are chasing an alien craft. The Rangers sit at the star-ship's controls.

| | |
|---|---|
| **Narrator** | Star Rangers patrol the stars, always ready for danger. |
| **Captain** | Come on, E.D. Faster. He's getting away. |
| **Narrator** | *(Engine sound)* VROOOM … |
| **Captain** | Fire blast guns! |
| **Narrator** | *(Guns)* BAM … BAM … |
| **Kaput** | Missed him. Faster, E.D. Faster! |
| **E.D.** | Beep-boop … alien returning fire. |
| **Narrator** | *(Guns)* ZAPP … BLAMMM … |
| **Kaput** | He hit us! |
| **E.D.** | Boop-beep … we have a hole in the hull … and engine damage. |
| **Kaput** | The alien got away! You lost him, E.D. |
| **Captain** | You're too slow, E.D. We need a new droid. |
| **Kaput** | And a new star-ship. This old tub's past it. |
| **Captain** | Rubbish! This star-ship's in mint condition. |
| **Kaput** | Yes, it's got a hole through the middle. |
| **E.D.** | Beep-boop … so has number one engine. The power drive is smashed. |

| Captain | We need a new star crystal to fix it. |
|---|---|
| Kaput | Where will we get a new star crystal? |
| E.D. | Boop-beep … from the planet Santos. |
| Kaput | The Santons are not very friendly. |
| Captain | It's our only chance. Get us there, E.D. Let's hope the other engine holds out. |

## SCENE 2

*Santos, a dark and gloomy planet. The Rangers are in a huge cave. Crystals shine from the rocks.*

*(Enter Cosmic and Kaput.)*

| Kaput | Look, Captain, loads of crystals. |
|---|---|
| Captain | OK, Kaput, grab one and let's get out of here. Where's E.D.? |
| Kaput | He'll be along soon. He's in a huff because we want a new droid. |

*(Enter Santon guards.)*

| Santon 1 | Hey! What are you doing in the crystal cave? |
|---|---|

| | |
|---|---|
| **Kaput** | Look out, Captain! |
| | *(All draw blaster guns and fire.)* |
| **Narrator** | *(Blasters)* BAM … ZZAP … ZZAP … |
| **Kaput** | There's too many of them, Captain. |
| **Narrator** | *(Blasters)* ZZAP … BAM … |
| **Captain** | Stop firing. We give up. |
| **Santon 2** | Drop your weapons. |
| **Santon 1** | Who are you? |
| **Captain** | We're Star Rangers. Our star-ship has been damaged. We need a star crystal to fix the engine. |
| **Santon 2** | The crystals belong to the Santons. Anyone who takes a crystal will be punished by death. |
| **Kaput** | Oops! I bet that hurts. |
| | *(Enter E.D. He does not see the Santons.)* |
| **E.D.** | Beep-boop … Captain, did you find the crystals? Oh, excuse me … |
| **Captain** | Get back E.D. They've got blaster guns! |
| | *(Santons drop their blasters and kneel.)* |
| **Santon 2** | It is Bika! Bika has come at last! |

| | |
|---|---|
| **Santon 1** | Bika! Bika! |
| **Kaput** | What's going on, Captain? |
| **Captain** | They must think E.D.'s some sort of god. |
| **Santon 2** | Do not be angry, Bika. |
| **Santon 1** | We came to stop these creatures taking the crystals. |
| **Santon 2** | What shall we do with them, Bika? |
| **E.D.** | Boop-beep … cover them in peanut butter and fry them alive. |
| **Captain** | *(Gulps)* Look, E.D., don't be cross. We don't really need a new droid. You're the best. |
| **Kaput** | Sorry, E.D. Please don't fry me in peanut butter. |
| **E.D.** | Beep-boop … guards, you must help me. |
| **Santon 1** | Yes, Bika. |
| **E.D.** | Boop-beep … give me a crystal. |
| | (Guard gives crystal to E.D.) |
| **E.D.** | Beep-boop … now, all guards must hold hands and stand on one leg. |
| **Santon 1** <br> **Santon 2** | Yes, Bika. |

| | |
|---|---|
| **E.D.** | Boop-beep … then close your eyes and count to ten. |
| **Santon 1** <br> **Santon 2** | 1 … 2 … 3 … |
| **E.D.** | Beep-boop … now, Captain! Let's beam up, let's get away! |
| | *(Exit Rangers.)* |
| **Santon 1** <br> **Santon 2** | … 8 … 9 … 10. |
| **Santon 1** | Bika … hello … where are you? |
| **Santon 2** | He's gone! He's taken the creatures to fry them alive. |

## SCENE 3

Back aboard the star-ship. The Rangers are at the controls.

| | |
|---|---|
| **Captain** | You gave us a fright, E.D. |
| **Kaput** | Sorry, E.D. We don't really need a new droid. |
| **E.D.** | Boop-beep … It's OK. We have the crystal. Now here's something to eat. |
| **Captain** | Yes please, E.D. What is it? |
| **E.D.** | Beep-boop … peanut butter sandwiches. |
| **Kaput** | No thanks, E.D. Suddenly I'm not hungry. |

# Star Wards

| Characters | |
|---|---|
| **Captain Cosmic** – Star Ranger | **Nurse** |
| **Kaput** – Star Ranger | **Doctor** |
| **E.D.** – Electro Droid | **Feelo Blonk** – Alien |

**Captain**  Star Rangers patrol the Galaxy, keeping space safe, always ready for danger.

## SCENE 1

*The Star Rangers' star-ship. The Rangers are sitting around the control deck.*

**Captain**  Space can be very boring.

**Kaput**  *Very* boring, Captain.

**Captain**  There are some wires sticking out of the control panel, Kaput. Push them back in.

**Kaput**  Yes, sir.

(Kaput prods wires ... FLASH ... ZZZ ... BANG ...)

**Kaput**  Yeeow ... OOO ... Captain ... OOO ...

**Captain**  What's the matter, Kaput?

**Kaput**  I got a shock from those wires. Now I've got a splitting headache. Have we got anything for it?

**E.D.**  Beep-boop ... have you tried glue?

**Kaput**  And I think I've lost my memory.

**Captain**  When did that happen?

**Kaput**  When did what happen?

**E.D.**  Boop-beep ... when did you lose your memory?

**Kaput**  I don't know. I forgot.

**Captain**  This is serious, E.D., I'm taking Kaput to hospital. I don't like the look of him.

**E.D.**  Beep-boop ... I'll come with you. I don't like to look at him either.

**Captain**  OK, E.D. To hospital. Maximum speed.

**E.D.**  Boop-beep ... let's go!

## SCENE 2

*A hospital star-ship. Enter Cosmic, Kaput and E.D. Aliens sit waiting for the doctor.*

| | |
|---|---|
| **Captain** | Look. This place is full of aliens. |
| **Kaput** | Yes, look at that green alien over there. He's got no nose. |
| **Captain** | Really? How does he smell? |
| **Kaput** | Awful! |
| **Feelo** | Hey! Who are you calling awful? |
| **Kaput** | Sorry. I didn't mean you. I meant me. *I* feel awful. |
| | *(Enter Nurse.)* |
| **Captain** | Nurse, Nurse. We need a doctor. |
| **Nurse** | I can see that. What's that nasty lump on your neck? |
| **E.D.** | Beep-boop … It's his head. |
| **Kaput** | Excuse me, Nurse, it's *me* that needs the doctor. |
| **Nurse** | What's the matter? |
| **Kaput** | I lost my memory. |
| **Nurse** | When did that happen? |
| **Kaput** | When did what happen? |

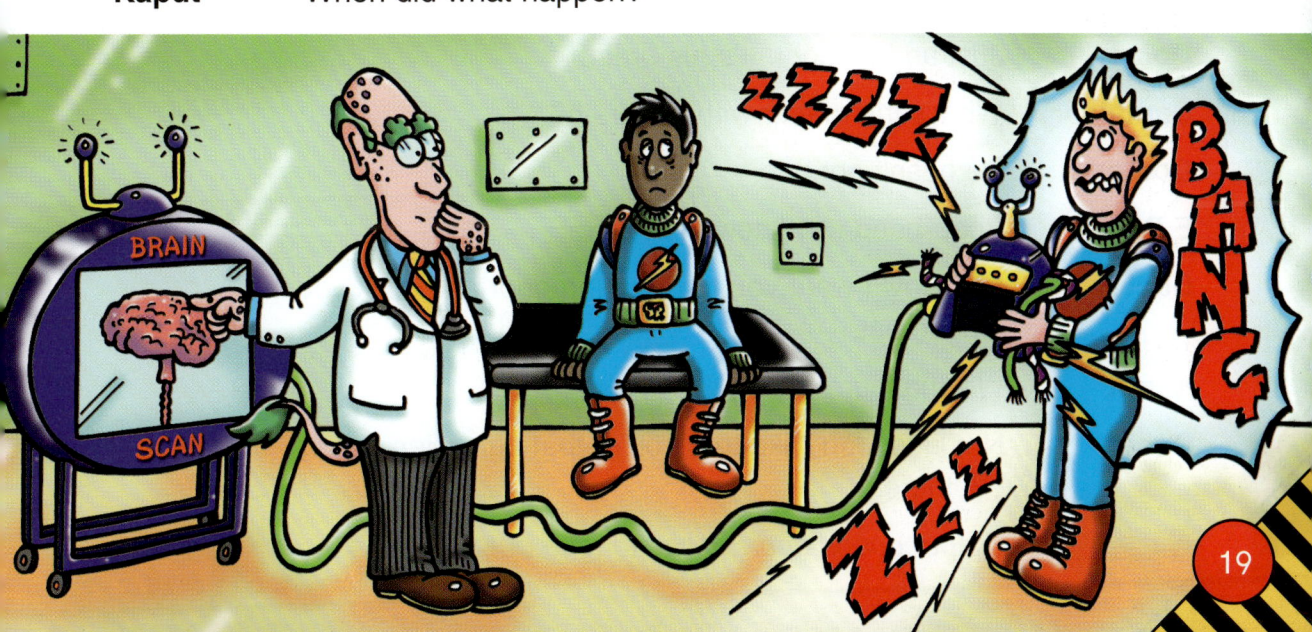

| | |
|---|---|
| **E.D.** | Boop-beep … he's off again. Get him to a doctor. |
| | *(Enter Doctor.)* |
| **Doctor** | Next, please. |
| | *(They enter the Doctor's room.)* |
| **Doctor** | Come in. I want to have a good look at you. Captain, hand me that brain scanner. Be careful. Don't touch those wires. |
| **Captain** | Do you mean *these* wires? |
| | *(Captain touches wires … ZZZZZZ … BANG …)* |
| **Captain** | Ow! Ooo! That hurt! |
| **Doctor** | Tell me, what's the problem? |
| **Captain** | Kaput has lost his memory. |
| **Doctor** | When did that happen? |
| **Captain** | When did what happen? |
| **E.D.** | Beep-boop … oh, no. Now the Captain's lost *his* memory. |
| **Doctor** | OK, Kaput. I'll give you a brain scan. Stick this scanner on your head. |
| | *(Doctor puts scanner on Kaput … ZZZZZZZZZ …)* |
| **Kaput** | Aagh! Ow! Ooh! |
| **Doctor** | Just as I thought. It's his brain. |
| **Captain** | What's the matter with his brain? |
| **Doctor** | He hasn't got one. |
| **E.D.** | Boop-beep … I knew it! |
| **Doctor** | OK. Now I want you to open the door and stick your tongue out. |
| **Kaput** | Will that cure me? |
| **Doctor** | No, I just don't like the look of that ugly alien sitting out there. |
| | *(Kaput opens door. Sticks tongue out at Feelo.)* |

| | |
|---|---|
| **Feelo** | Hey, you! Don't stick your tongue out at me. Wait till I get hold of you! |
| | *(Feelo grabs Kaput and lifts him up.)* |
| **Kaput** | Aagh! Put me down. That hurts! |
| **Captain** | Hey, you! Alien! Let go of his arm. Put him down. |
| | *(Feelo swings Kaput round.)* |
| **Kaput** | Yaaaargh!! |
| **E.D.** | Beep-boop … quick, Captain. Stick the brain scanner on the alien's head. |
| **Captain** | Good thinking, E.D. Here goes … |
| | *(Captain puts scanner on Feelo … ZZZZZZZZ …)* |
| **Feelo** | Yeow! Aagh! Ouch! |
| | *(Feelo drops Kaput.)* |
| **Kaput** | YES! I'm free! |
| **Feelo** | Ooh! Ooh! |
| | *(Enter Nurse.)* |
| **Nurse** | What's going on here? |
| **Doctor** | There's been a fight, Nurse. |
| **Nurse** | A fight? A fight in the Doctor's room! It's terrible! How did this happen? |
| **Captain** **Kaput** **Feelo** } | How did what happen? |
| **E.D.** | Beep-boop … oh-oh! |

# Close Encounters

> **Characters**
>
> **Captain Cosmic** – Star Ranger      **Monster**
> **Kaput** – Star Ranger      **Narrator**
> **E.D.** – Electro Droid      **Sound Effects** – SFX

## SCENE 1

*The Star Rangers' star-ship. The Rangers sit at the controls.*

| | |
|---|---|
| **Narrator** | Space – the final frontier … Star Rangers – patrolling the stars, keeping the Galaxy secure. |
| **SFX** | *(Alarm)* Woop … woop … |
| **E.D.** | Beep-boop … incoming transmission from Star Base, Captain. |
| **Captain** | Put it on the answer machine. I'm having a nap. |
| **Kaput** | It's a code three transmission, sir. Ultra-important. |
| **Captain** | But my nap is ultra-important too! |
| **SFX** | *(Radio voice)* Cosmic! This is the Chief Ranger. |
| **Captain** | Oops! Yes, sir. Cosmic here, sir. |
| **SFX** | *(Radio voice)* Cosmic! What's your position? |
| **Captain** | Upright, sir. Sitting in a chair. |
| **SFX** | *(Radio voice)* Not *your* position, you spaced-out twit. What's your *ship's* position? |
| **Captain** | Sorry, sir. Kaput, what's our position? |
| **Kaput** | We're approaching the planet Zigos. |
| **SFX** | *(Radio voice)* Excellent! We've got a problem in the asteroid belt beyond Zigos. One of our envoys is missing. We think some space monster got him. Check it out. |

| | |
|---|---|
| **Captain** | Yes, sir! Immediately! |
| **Kaput** | OK, E.D. Find those asteroids. Maximum thrust. |
| **Narrator** | So the Rangers' ship skimmed past Zigos, and then … |
| **E.D.** | Boop-beep … asteroids ahead. |
| **Captain** | Can you see anything, Kaput? |
| **Kaput** | Just a load of rocks, sir. |
| **E.D.** | Beep-boop … sensors are picking up a life form, Captain, from that large asteroid. Shall we beam down? |
| **Kaput** | It looks a bit spooky and dangerous. |
| **Captain** | Danger is our business, Kaput. We're Star Rangers. It's all for one and one for all. |
| **Kaput** | Good! If it's one for all, maybe just one of us should beam down. I vote for E.D. |
| **Captain** | Come on, Rangers. When the going gets tough, the tough get going! |

## SCENE 2

*The asteroid.*

**Narrator**  So the Rangers took their positions on the transporter pads, then beamed down to the asteroid.

*(Enter Star Rangers.)*

**Kaput**  You see? There's no-one here. Let's go back.

**Captain**  Hold it. There *is* something here. I can smell it.

**Kaput**  I think that's me, sir.

**E.D.**  Boop-beep … sensors show a lifeform approaching.

**Captain**  OK, men. Weapons ready.

**Kaput**  Where is it E.D.? Where is it?

**E.D.**  Beep-boop … sensors show it's … behind us!

*(Enter Monster.)*

**Monster**  YAAAARGH!!

**Kaput**  Aaargh! Run! Monster!

**Captain**  Stand firm, Rangers. Weapons ready … fire!

**SFX**  *(Weapons)* ZZUG … ZZUG …

**Monster**  YAAARGH!

**Kaput**  It's no good. Our weapons are useless.

**Monster**  YAAARGH!

**Captain**  OK, cease firing. E.D., use your language transponder. See if we can talk to it.

**E.D.**  Boop-beep … transponder engaged, Captain. Go ahead.

**Captain**  *(Shouts)* HELLO, SPACE MONSTER. CAN YOU HEAR ME?

**Monster**  YAARGH! Of course I can hear you. There's no need to shout.

| | |
|---|---|
| **Captain** | Sorry! I'm Captain Cosmic. We're Star Rangers. We come in peace. |
| **Monster** | In peace?! You nearly had me in pieces. Those weapons really sting. |
| **Kaput** | Sorry, but you gave us a fright when you jumped out going "Yaargh, yaargh". |
| **Monster** | I'm a monster. I'm supposed to go "Yaargh, yaargh". |
| **Captain** | We're looking for our envoy. He disappeared somewhere around here. |
| **Monster** | Was that the little chap with the moustache? Was he called Norman? |
| **E.D.** | Beep-boop … checking data … confirmed. |
| **Monster** | Yes, he came here. He was very nice. |
| **Captain** | You saw him? |
| **Monster** | Yes, I was glad of the company. It gets very lonely here. |
| **Kaput** | So, where is he now? |
| **Monster** | I ate him. |
| **Captain** | You ate him?! |

**Kaput**       Why did you eat him?

**Monster**     Hey! Look around this place. It's rocks, rocks and more rocks. Nothing to eat. I can't send out for a pizza here. I got hungry so I ate him.

**Captain**     Well, I suppose that's that. If he's gone we can't bring him back.

**Kaput**       No, we'd better just beam back to the ship.

**Monster**     *(Gurgle, gurgle)*

**E.D.**        Boop-beep … I'm picking up a noise.

**Monster**     It's my stomach. I'm hungry again. Mmm! You look very juicy.

**Kaput**       Oh, no! Why couldn't we meet a vegetarian monster.

**Captain**     E.D.! Think of something fast!

**E.D.**        Beep-boop … this monster is from a species that originates from Zigos, Captain.

**Captain**     I know, why don't we take you back to Zigos. There's loads to eat there.

**Monster**     That's very kind of you.

**Captain**     We can use our tractor beam to lift you down to the planet.

**Monster**     Wonderful! I'm so grateful.

**Narrator**    So the Star Rangers blasted off, towing the monster behind them. And when they got to Zigos, they dropped him off …

**Monster**     Ouch!

**Narrator**    … And then they streaked away across the stars, another day done, another mission over …
                … pity about Norman, of course, but …

**Captain**     Star Rangers are GO!

# 3001 – A Space Oddity

> ## Characters
>
> **Captain Cosmic** – Star Ranger      **Varg** – Leader of Dark Force
> **Kaput** – Star Ranger      **Narrator 1**
> **E.D.** – Electro Droid      **Narrator 2/Sound Effects**

## SCENE

*The Star Rangers' star-ship. The Rangers are at the controls.*

**Narrator 1**  Once upon a time, in a galaxy far away, Star Rangers patrolled the planets, keeping space safe.

**E.D.**  Beep-boop … Captain, I'm picking up a distress signal from the Mia Quadrant.

**Narrator 2**  *(Distress signal)* DAT … DAT … DAT …

**Kaput**  It must be from a star-ship.

**Captain**  Get us there, E.D. Maximum thrust!

**Narrator 1**  So the Star Rangers streaked towards the dark and distant Mia Quadrant.

**Kaput**  It looks like trouble, Captain. I hope it's not Varg.

**Captain**  No chance. Varg is on the run on the other side of the Galaxy.

**Narrator 1**  The evil Varg wants to conquer the Galaxy.

**Narrator 2**  Only the Star Rangers can stop him, so Varg has vowed to exterminate all Star Rangers – every last one …

**Kaput**  OK, this is it, this is where the signal is coming from.

**Narrator 1**  But there was nothing to be seen. Just the black emptiness of space … Then …

*(Kaput peers through the cabin window.)*

**Kaput**  Captain. What's that? … Look … out there!

| | |
|---|---|
| **Captain** | It's a small black slab. E.D., can you get a sensor reading on it? |
| **E.D.** | Boop-beep … my sensors do not recognise the object, but that's where the signal is coming from. |
| **Captain** | Beam it on board. |
| **Narrator 2** | *(Sound of beam)* ZZZZZZ … |
| | *(A small black slab appears on the floor of the starship.)* |
| **Kaput** | Look, Captain. It's not very big. |
| **Captain** | So why the distress signal? It's just a black slab. |
| | *(Cosmic and Kaput approach the slab.)* |
| **E.D.** | Beep-boop … be careful. It might be a trap. |
| **Kaput** | Look. There's something printed on it – '3001'. |
| **Captain** | '3001'? Very odd! Is that a key-pad set in the top? |
| **E.D.** | Boop-beep … perhaps '3001' is a code. Type it into the key-pad. |
| **Kaput** | I'll try it. *(Types)* 3 … 0 … 0 … 1. |
| **Narrator 1** | A low hum filled the air. Suddenly the slab began to open up and unfold … |

**Narrator 2** From the opened slab rose a shimmering silver light, and from that light stepped the dark figure of a man … Varg!

*(Enter Varg.)*

**Varg** Ah, Cosmic! How helpful of you. Thank you for releasing me.

**Captain** Varg! I thought you were finished!

| | |
|---|---|
| **Varg** | No, Cosmic! I have returned to finish *you*! |
| **Kaput** | But where have you come from? |
| **Varg** | Ah, yes. Let me introduce you to my star-gate, my portal. With this device I can travel the stars undetected. Once the portal is opened I can step from one end of the Galaxy to the other. |
| **Captain** | Very clever, Varg, but what do you want? |
| **Varg** | I want *you*, Cosmic. I want your secret codes. |
| **Captain** | I will never give up the codes, and neither will my men. |
| **Varg** | How many on board? |
| **Captain** | Just Kaput and myself. |
| | *(Varg points to E.D.)* |
| **Varg** | What's that? |
| **Kaput** | That's E.D. |
| **Captain** | It's a rubbish machine. We use it to get rid of rubbish. |
| **E.D.** | Beep-boop … rubbish like you, Varg. |
| **Varg** | Who said that? Who said I was rubbish? |
| **Kaput** | It wasn't me! I didn't hear anything, did you, Captain? |
| **Captain** | You're imagining it, Varg. |
| **Varg** | There's someone else here! |
| | *(Varg checks around. Cosmic turns to E.D.)* |
| **Captain** | *(Whispers)* E.D., what are you doing? |
| **E.D.** | Boop-beep … I want Varg to come over here, Captain. I've switched my stun shield on. If he touches me the shield will knock him out. |
| **Kaput** | *(Whispers)* Look out, Captain. He's coming back. |
| **Varg** | What's going on, Cosmic? Are you trying to make a fool of me? |
| **E.D.** | Beep-boop … he doesn't need to try, you twit! |

**Varg**        It's that rubbish machine. It called me a twit. I'm going to rip its circuits out!

            (Varg grabs E.D.)

**Narrator 2**   (Sound of sparks) KRAK … KRAK …

| | |
|---|---|
| **Varg** | Aaagh! |
| | *(Varg falls back. Cosmic and Kaput grab him.)* |
| **Captain** | Drag him onto the portal, Kaput! |
| | *(Varg falls onto the portal.)* |
| **Kaput** | What do we do now!? |
| **E.D.** | Boop-beep … the key-pad … type the code number quickly. |
| | *(Varg struggles.)* |
| **Varg** | Aagh! I'm going to exterminate you. |
| | *(Kaput types the code.)* |
| **Kaput** | 3 … 0 … 0 …1. |
| **Captain** | Nothing! It's not working! |
| **E.D.** | Beep-boop … reverse the number. |
| **Kaput** | Good thinking, E.D. *(Types)* 1 … 0 … 0 … 3. |
| **Narrator 2** | *(Sound of portal)* HMMMMMMM … |
| **Captain** | It's working! Look! |
| **Narrator 1** | The air around the portal began to shimmer. Then the evil form of Varg turned to a shadow and slowly disappeared. |
| **Varg** | I'll be back, Star Rangers … I'll be back … |
| | *(Exit Varg.)* |
| **Captain** | We'll be ready, Varg. Ready and waiting. We are … STAR RANGERS! |